RICHARD OLNEY

Cooking For Two

Photography by SIMON WHEELER

THE MASTER CHEFS

TED SMART

RICHARD OLNEY was born in Iowa and studied at the University of Iowa and at Brooklyn Museum Art School. He has lived in France since 1951, and moved to Provence in 1961.

He writes about food and wine for magazines in America and Britain, and between 1963 and 1980 he was a regular contributor to *Cuisine et Vins de France* and *La Revue du Vin de France*.

He was the consultant editor of the 27-volume Time-Life series, *The Good Cook*, and is the author of many books, including *The French Menu Cookbook*, *Simple French Food*, *Yquem*, *Ten Vineyard Lunches*, *Romanée-Conti*, *Provence The Beautiful Cookbook* and *Lulu's Provençal Table*.

CONTENTS

Faites simple.

ESCOFFIER

INTRODUCTION

The recipes that follow have been chosen with inexpensive ingredients in mind, for the simplicity of execution, the beauty of presentation...and because my guests always love them. Each is a variation on a theme, intended to teach basic mechanics or principles and to liberate creative impulses. Consider, for instance, adding a *chiffonade* of spinach, chard or sorrel to the vegetable soup or, a few minutes before serving, a handful of little peas or tender young broad beans. Parboiled, squeezed, chopped and sautéed spinach – or sautéed onions, potatoes and *persillade* – can replace the courgettes in a flat omelette. Birds can be stuffed beneath the skin with myriad mixtures (because of their bulk, chickens and guinea fowl are more easily baked in the oven for about 1 hour). As for the salad, potatoes marry with almost anything but, unless they are peeled hot and added immediately to the vinaigrette – and unless the vinaigrette is made from perfect vinegar, olive oil, salt and pepper – your salad will be banal.

VEGETABLE SOUP

1 LITRE/1¾ PINTS WATER

COARSE SEA SALT

1 SPRIG OF THYME

1 BAY LEAF

2 GARLIC CLOVES, SLICED

2 SMALL CARROTS, ABOUT 125 G/
    4 OZ, SLICED

1 LEEK, ABOUT 150 G/5 OZ, WHITE
    AND PALE GREEN PARTS, SLIT,
    SOAKED IN COLD WATER, THEN
    FINELY SLICED

1–2 POTATOES, ABOUT 225 G/8 OZ,
    QUARTERED AND SLICED

1 ONION, FINELY SLICED

1 COURGETTE, SLICED INTO
    WEDGES

50 G/2 OZ SPAGHETTI OR
    SPAGHETTINI, BROKEN UP

ABOUT 100 G/3½ OZ GREEN
    BEANS, TOPPED AND TAILED, THEN
    SLICED INTO PEA-SIZE LENGTHS

TO SERVE

FRESHLY GROUND BLACK PEPPER

A WEDGE OF PARMESAN CHEESE

EXTRA VIRGIN OLIVE OIL

Put the water, salt, herbs and garlic in a large saucepan over medium-high heat. As you prepare them, add the carrots, leek, potatoes and onion. When the water boils, partially cover the pan and adjust the heat to maintain a light boil.

After 20 minutes, add the courgette and the pasta, stirring with a wooden spoon. After a further 5 minutes, stir in the green beans. Cook for 7–8 minutes longer or until the pasta is tender (not *al dente*). Serve in warmed soup plates.

At table, grind some black pepper over the soup, grate some cheese on top and drizzle with olive oil.

PUMPKIN AND MUSSEL SOUP

15 G/½ OZ UNSALTED BUTTER
1 SMALL ONION, FINELY CHOPPED
ABOUT 450 G/1 LB PUMPKIN OR
    OTHER ORANGE-FLESHED
    WINTER SQUASH, THICKLY
    PEELED, SEEDED AND DICED
COARSE SEA SALT
450 G/1 LB MUSSELS, OPENED IN
    WHITE WINE (PAGE 30)
4 TABLESPOONS DOUBLE CREAM

TO SERVE
CROÛTONS (PAGE 29)
FRESHLY GROUND BLACK PEPPER

Melt the butter in a heavy saucepan over low heat, add the onion, cover the pan and cook until softened but not coloured. Add the pumpkin, a little salt (the mussels' cooking liquid may be more or less salty) and continue to cook over low heat, covered, for about 30 minutes, stirring occasionally with a wooden spoon.

Add the mussels' cooking liquid, bring to the boil and simmer, partially covered, until the pumpkin is so tender it is almost a purée.

If necessary, add a little water to lighten the body of the soup. Taste and add more salt if required. Strain the soup through a sieve and bring it back to the boil. Add the mussels, stir in the cream and serve at once, in warmed soup plates. Scatter the surface with croûtons and grind some black pepper over the soup at table.

SCRAMBLED EGGS
with asparagus

1 GARLIC CLOVE, PEELED

45 G/1½ OZ COLD UNSALTED
    BUTTER, DICED

6 EGGS

SALT AND FRESHLY GROUND BLACK
    PEPPER

225 G/½ LB ASPARAGUS, STEMS
    PEELED, SLICED THINLY ON THE
    DIAGONAL, PARBOILED IN
    HEAVILY SALTED WATER FOR A
    FEW SECONDS ONLY, THEN
    DRAINED

CROÛTONS (PAGE 29)

*The eggs are cooked in a bain-marie;
I use a heavy saucepan placed on a
trivet in a larger saucepan that is filled
with water to about the level of the
eggs in the smaller pan. To gauge the
amount of water, assemble the pans and
trivet in advance.*

Rub a wooden spoon with the
garlic. Butter the smaller saucepan.
Place 15 g/½ oz of the butter in a
bowl, break over the eggs, season
and beat lightly with a fork.

Pour the eggs into the smaller
saucepan, place it on the trivet in
the larger pan and heat until the
water is nearly boiling. Keeping the
water just below the boil, stir the
eggs slowly and regularly with the
garlicky spoon, scraping the sides,
corners and bottom of the pan.

Melt 15 g/½ oz butter in an
omelette pan and sauté the
parboiled asparagus over high heat,
just long enough to heat through.
Stir into the eggs.

As the eggs begin to thicken,
watch them closely, stirring more
rapidly. As they approach a creamy
but pourable consistency, remove
the pan from the water. Add the
remaining butter and stir for half a
minute. Serve in warmed plates and
scatter with croûtons.

FLAT COURGETTE OMELETTE

2 FIRM COURGETTES, ABOUT
   325 G/12 OZ
SALT
2 TABLESPOONS OLIVE OIL
15 G/½ OZ COLD UNSALTED
   BUTTER, DICED
1 TABLESPOON LEAVES AND
   UNOPENED FLOWER BUDS OF
   TENDER FRESH MARJORAM,
   FINELY CHOPPED
3 EGGS
FRESHLY GROUND BLACK PEPPER
HANDFUL OF FRESHLY GRATED
   PARMESAN CHEESE

Shred the courgettes with the
medium shredding blade of a food
processor, or grate them coarsely.
Layer the shreds in a bowl,
sprinkling each layer with salt, and
leave for at least 30 minutes.
Squeeze tightly and transfer to a
plate, discarding the liquid.

Heat the grill. Heat half the
olive oil in an omelette pan, add
the courgettes and sauté for 2–3
minutes, until lightly coloured.

Put the butter and marjoram in
a bowl with the eggs, salt and
pepper. Stir with a fork and add
the courgettes, stirring briskly.

Replace the pan over high heat,
add the remaining oil, swirl to coat
the pan and add the egg mixture.
Stir with the fork, tines facing up,
without scraping the pan, for about
30 seconds. Sprinkle the cheese
over the omelette, taking care not
to touch the pan.

Place the pan under the hot
grill for 1–2 minutes or until the
eggs are nearly set at the centre.
Shake the pan gently, to be certain
the omelette slips freely, and slide it
on to a warmed platter. Serve cut
into wedges.

COMPOSED SALAD

2 EGGS
275 G/10 OZ SMALL, FIRM-FLESHED
  POTATOES
HANDFUL OF SMALL GREEN BEANS,
  TOPPED, TAILED AND CUT INTO
  2.5 CM/1 INCH SECTIONS
HANDFUL OF BLACK OLIVES
4 SALTED ANCHOVIES, BRIEFLY
  SOAKED IN COLD WATER,
  FILLETED, RINSED, PATTED DRY
  BETWEEN PAPER TOWELS
1 TABLESPOON FINELY CHOPPED
  FLAT-LEAF PARSLEY

VINAIGRETTE

SALT AND FRESHLY GROUND BLACK
  PEPPER
1 TABLESPOON RED WINE VINEGAR
3 TABLESPOONS OLIVE OIL
1 SHALLOT, VERY FINELY CHOPPED

Place the eggs in a saucepan of cold water, bring to the boil and simmer for 9 minutes. Immerse in a bowl of cold water and set aside.

Boil the potatoes in their skins until just done, about 25 minutes.

While the potatoes are cooking, prepare the vinaigrette. Grind salt and pepper into the salad bowl, add the vinegar, swirl it to dissolve the salt, add the olive oil and stir in the shallot with a salad serving spoon and fork.

Cook the beans in boiling water until barely tender, 2–5 minutes. Drain, but do not refresh in cold water.

Drain the potatoes and peel them while still boiling hot, protecting your hands with a tea towel. Slice them directly into the vinaigrette and toss them immediately – only when hot will they absorb its flavours correctly.

Shell the eggs and slice thinly over the potatoes – the yolks will crumble coarsely. Scatter over the beans, olives, anchovies and parsley, in that order. Present the salad before tossing it at table.

GRILLED SPLIT QUAIL
stuffed beneath the skin

2 QUAIL

OLIVE OIL

PINCH OF MIXED DRIED HERBS
  (PAGE 29)

SALT AND FRESHLY GROUND BLACK
  PEPPER

STUFFING

1 TABLESPOON OLIVE OIL

125 G/4 OZ MUSHROOMS, FINELY
  CHOPPED

PERSILLADE (PAGE 29)

½ LEMON

SMALL HANDFUL OF FRESH
  BREADCRUMBS

15 G/½ OZ UNSALTED BUTTER,
  SOFTENED

First make the stuffing. Heat the oil in a frying pan, add the mushrooms, season and toss until the liquid they render has reduced and the pan is nearly dry. Add the persillade, toss until its scent fills the room, then squeeze over a few drops of lemon juice. Scrape the mushrooms into a bowl and leave to cool. Using a fork, mash together the mushrooms, breadcrumbs and softened butter. Refrigerate until firm.

Prepare and stuff the quail (page 30).

Heat the grill or a barbecue over wood embers. Drizzle olive oil over the birds, gently rubbing it over all surfaces. Sprinkle the herbs, salt and pepper over the birds, then grill them, underside first, for 7–8 minutes. Turn them to grill the skin side for 5 minutes (take care – the skin burns easily), then turn them back to finish grilling – about 18 minutes in all. Serve accompanied by sautéed or fried potatoes.

BAKED RABBIT,
sorrel cream sauce

½ RABBIT, CUT INTO SERVING
  PIECES (2 LEGS, 2 SADDLE
  SECTIONS)

275 G/10 OZ SMALL, FIRM-FLESHED
  POTATOES, PEELED

1 HEAD OF NEW GARLIC, CLOVES
  PEELED (ELIMINATE IF OUT OF
  SEASON)

LARGE HANDFUL OF TENDER
  SORREL CHIFFONADE (PAGE 29)

COARSE SEA SALT

JUICE OF ½ LEMON

1 TABLESPOON DIJON MUSTARD

125 ML/4 FL OZ DOUBLE CREAM

MARINADE

1 TEASPOON MIXED DRIED HERBS
  (PAGE 29)

1 BAY LEAF

1 ONION, SLICED

1 TABLESPOON OLIVE OIL

SMALL GLASS OF DRY WHITE WINE

First marinate the rabbit. Sprinkle the rabbit pieces with the herbs and place in a bowl with the bay leaf, onion, oil and wine. Leave to marinate for about 3 hours, turning twice.

Preheat the oven to 200°C/ 400°F/Gas Mark 6. Fit the rabbit pieces, potatoes and garlic cloves into an ovenproof dish just large enough to hold them in a single layer. Strain the marinade and add the onion and bay leaf to the dish. Scatter the sorrel chiffonade over the surface and sprinkle with salt.

Mix together the strained marinade, lemon juice, mustard and cream, spoon about half over the rabbit and bake for 1 hour, basting with the remaining cream mixture two or three times after the first 30 minutes. When the surface begins to colour, reduce the oven temperature to 180°C/350°F/Gas Mark 4 and cover the dish with foil. Serve hot, on warmed plates.

BRAISED STUFFED SQUID

3 TABLESPOONS OLIVE OIL

1 ONION, FINELY CHOPPED

2 MEDIUM-LARGE SQUID (POUCHES
    ABOUT 20 CM/8 INCHES LONG),
    CLEANED (PAGE 30), WINGS AND
    TENTACLES CHOPPED

PINCH OF SAFFRON STIGMAS

SALT AND FRESHLY GROUND BLACK
    PEPPER

CAYENNE PEPPER

HANDFUL (ABOUT 85 G/3 OZ) OF
    LONG-GRAIN RICE, PARBOILED
    FOR 15 MINUTES, RINSED
    UNDER COLD WATER AND
    DRAINED WELL

450 G/1 LB MUSSELS, OPENED IN
    WHITE WINE (PAGE 30)

PERSILLADE (PAGE 29)

3 SALTED ANCHOVIES, SOAKED,
    FILLETED AND CHOPPED

ABOUT 2 TABLESPOONS COGNAC

Heat 1 tablespoon of the oil in a small frying pan, add half the onion and cook until softened but not coloured. Add the chopped squid wings and tentacles, saffron, salt, pepper and cayenne, turn up the heat and cook, stirring, until the squid juices have been released and reduced to about 1 tablespoon. Mix with the rice and half the mussels. Fill the pouches (not too tightly) and close with a trussing needle and kitchen string.

In a small, heavy sauté pan over low heat, cook the rest of the onion in the remaining oil until softened. Increase the heat, add the persillade, anchovies and stuffed squid; roll the pouches around until the flesh has contracted. Add the brandy and cook, shaking the pan, until the liquid has almost disappeared. Add mussel broth to about 5 mm/¼ inch, cover tightly and simmer over very low heat for 50 minutes; add more mussel broth if necessary.

Add the remaining mussels to warm through. Remove the string from the pouches and serve on warmed plates.

BRAISED SWEETBREADS
with little peas

2 LOBES OF VEAL SWEETBREADS,
    ABOUT 450 G/1 LB
25 G/1 OZ UNSALTED BUTTER
BOUQUET GARNI (PAGE 29)
HANDFUL OF SMALL WHITE ONIONS,
    PEELED
COARSE SEA SALT
450 G/1 LB FRESHLY PICKED LITTLE
    PEAS, SHELLED
PINCH OF SUGAR
HANDFUL OF LETTUCE CHIFFONADE
    (PAGE 29)
1 TABLESPOON WATER

Soak the sweetbreads in cold water for 4–5 hours.

Place them in a large saucepan, cover with cold water, bring slowly to boiling point and keep them barely simmering over low heat for 15 minutes. Drain, refresh in cold water and peel them, removing superficial membranes and fat.

Butter a flameproof earthenware casserole and add the sweetbreads, bouquet garni and onions. Sprinkle with a little salt, add the peas, the remaining butter, cut into tiny dice, a little more salt and the sugar. Spread the lettuce chiffonade over the surface, sprinkle over a little water, cover tightly and cook over low heat for 45–50 minutes, shaking the casserole occasionally. Discard the bouquet garni and serve directly from the casserole.

GLAZED APPLE CRÊPE ROULADES

50 G/2 OZ UNSALTED BUTTER

3 NON-ACIDIC APPLES (FOR
    EXAMPLE, RUSSET OR COX'S
    PIPPINS), PEELED, QUARTERED,
    SEEDED AND SLICED

6 CRÊPES (PAGE 28)

SUGAR

Melt half the butter in a large frying pan, add the apples and sauté, tossing often, until they are soft and tender, but still intact.

Butter a gratin dish large enough to hold the rolled crêpes, side by side, without crowding. Roll a couple of tablespoons of sautéed apples in each crêpe and place it, seam-side down, in the dish. Place a strip of butter on each crêpe and sprinkle with sugar. The crêpes may be prepared up to this point 1–2 hours in advance.

Preheat the oven to 230°C/450°F/Gas Mark 8. Put the dish into the hot oven for about 10 minutes or until a light caramel glaze has formed on the surface of the crêpes. Serve hot, with a glass of fine Sauternes.

THE BASICS

CRÊPES

(use a small crêpe pan, 12 cm/5 inches in diameter)

1 SLIGHTLY MOUNDED TABLESPOON
  FLOUR
PINCH OF SALT
1 EGG
85 ML/3 FL OZ MILK
1 TABLESPOON COGNAC
15 G/½ OZ UNSALTED BUTTER,
  MELTED IN THE CRÊPE PAN

Sift the flour and salt into a bowl, add the egg and whisk from the centre outwards, gradually adding most of the milk, until all the flour is absorbed. Whisk in the brandy and melted butter. Add more milk if necessary to bring the batter to the consistency of double cream.

Wipe the crêpe pan with a paper towel to leave only a film of butter, and place it over medium to low heat. Remove the pan from the heat and rotate it as you pour in just enough batter from a small ladle to coat the bottom of the pan.

The batter should sizzle on contact. Return the pan to the heat. When the edges of the crêpe turn golden and curl up, slip a round-tipped knife beneath to flip it over. After a few seconds, slip the crêpe from the pan, using your fingertips.

Remove the pan from the heat for a few seconds between each crêpe to prevent it from becoming overheated, and give the batter a stir each time before ladling it out. The first side cooked is always the most evenly coloured and should be presented as the outside of a rolled crêpe. Stack the crêpes on a plate as they are finished.

A one-egg batter will produce more than enough crêpes for two. Cover the others with clingfilm and refrigerate for future use. If their congealed butter makes them stick together, warm the plate in a cool oven or over steam.

CROÛTONS

2 OR 3 SLICES OF FIRM-CRUMBED,
  SEMI-FRESH BREAD, 1 CM/
  ½ INCH THICK, CRUSTS
  REMOVED, CUT INTO DICE
15 G/½ OZ BUTTER

Melt the butter in an omelette pan over low heat, add the bread cubes and toss from time to time, adding more butter if the pan becomes dry. The croûtons are ready when they are golden (not brown) and crisp, but not dried out in the centre.

BOUQUET GARNI
A partially split section of leek and a piece of celery fit neatly together to enclose one or more sprigs of thyme, parsley stalks and a bay leaf, wound round tightly with kitchen string and tied. Try substituting winter savory or marjoram for thyme. In Provence, dried strips of orange zest are included for daubes and game stews.

CHIFFONADE *(finely shredded leaves)*
For lettuce, use a tender, round variety; wash the leaves, stack them on top of each other, roll up and cut across into fine ribbons. For spinach, chard or sorrel, use young leaves; pull off the stems, then roll up and shred.

PERSILLADE
Chop 1 clove garlic and the leaves from a small bunch of flat-leaf parsley. Gather together the garlic and parsley and chop finely until homogeneous.

MIXED DRIED HERBS
I use a mixture of wild thyme, picked in flower in April, oregano, picked in flower in July, marjoram, picked throughout the summer as it buds and begins to flower, and winter savory, picked in late summer. All are tied in bundles and hung to dry. In autumn, they are crumbled, sieved and stored in jars.

MUSSELS

Rinse in a bowl of cold water with a handful of sea salt. Scrub or scrape them, pull out the beards, and test each mussel by pressing between thumb and forefinger. Discard those that remain open, and any with broken shells.

In a large saucepan, assemble a sprig of thyme, a bay leaf, 1 tablespoon each of chopped celery and parsley, 1 small onion, finely chopped, 2 crushed garlic cloves, 15 g/½ oz butter and a small glass of white wine. Add the mussels, cover the pan tightly, place over high heat and shake regularly for 3–4 minutes or until the mussels are opened.

Empty the pan into a colander, collecting the cooking liquid in a bowl. Remove the mussels from their shells and strain the cooking liquid through a sieve lined with a double thickness of muslin. If not being used immediately, pour some of the liquid over the mussels to keep them moist.

SQUID

Pull the head and tentacles away from the pouch and pull out the clear, plastic-like 'pen'. Holding the head underwater, cut around and squeeze out the eyes and the beak. Rinse out the pouch. The violet-brown skin is often peeled off, but its presence may enhance the flavour.

TO STUFF A SMALL BIRD BENEATH THE SKIN

Applicable to farmed quail and partridge (hunted birds usually have damaged skin from shot). Cut off the bird's head, wingtips and feet. Slit the skin at the back of the neck, pull it free from the neck and loosen the trachea and oesophagus from the skin. Using poultry shears, split along the back, from tail to neck; remove the neck. Discard any innards. Open the bird out, inside facing down, and press hard on the breast with the heel of your hand to rupture the breastbone and ribcage.

Using your index and middle finger, reach through the neck opening to separate the breast skin from the flesh. Introduce the stuffing, a teaspoonful at a time, moulding the surface with your other hand. Fold the neck skin over the back to close the opening. With the tip of a knife, make a slit in the abdominal skin between the legs. Draw the legs up over the lower breast and tuck through the slit to pull the birds together in a neat, rounded form.

THE MASTER CHEFS

SOUPS
ARABELLA BOXER

MEZE, TAPAS AND ANTIPASTI
AGLAIA KREMEZI

PASTA SAUCES
GORDON RAMSAY

RISOTTO
MICHELE SCICOLONE

SALADS
CLARE CONNERY

MEDITERRANEAN
ANTONY WORRALL THOMPSON

VEGETABLES
PAUL GAYLER

LUNCHES
ALASTAIR LITTLE

COOKING FOR TWO
RICHARD OLNEY

FISH
RICK STEIN

CHICKEN
BRUNO LOUBET

SUPPERS
VALENTINA HARRIS

THE MAIN COURSE
ROGER VERGÉ

ROASTS
JANEEN SARLIN

WILD FOOD
ROWLEY LEIGH

PACIFIC
JILL DUPLEIX

CURRIES
PAT CHAPMAN

HOT AND SPICY
PAUL AND JEANNE RANKIN

THAI
JACKI PASSMORE

CHINESE
YAN-KIT SO

VEGETARIAN
KAREN LEE

DESSERTS
MICHEL ROUX

CAKES
CAROLE WALTER

COOKIES
ELINOR KLIVANS

THE MASTER CHEFS

This edition produced for The Book People Ltd,

Hall Wood Avenue, Haydock, St Helens WAII 9UL

Text © copyright 1996 Richard Olney

Photographs © copyright 1996 Simon Wheeler

First published in 1996 by

WEIDENFELD & NICOLSON

THE ORION PUBLISHING GROUP

ORION HOUSE

5 UPPER ST MARTIN'S LANE

LONDON WC2H 9EA

British Library Cataloguing-in-Publication data
A catalogue record for this book is available
from the British Library.

ISBN 0 297 83650 1

DESIGNED BY THE SENATE
EDITOR MAGGIE RAMSAY
FOOD STYLIST JOY DAVIES
ASSISTANT KATY HOLDER